PAXT

And the
BIG FLUFFY PILLOW

by Blaine Short
Illustrator Jean Mostert

Illustrations completed by Jean Mostert
Based on her 1972 character "BANANAS"

It had been a long day and Paxton was very tired.

The walk home was going very slowly, when Paxton declared he wanted a fluffy pillow!

Mom and Dad stopped to graze, so Paxton said it louder. "I want a fluffy pillow!"

Paxton decided he would just go find a fluffy pillow himself.

He tried a rock but it was too hard.

"I want a fluffy pillow." He cried.

He tried a pile of grass but it made him sneeze!

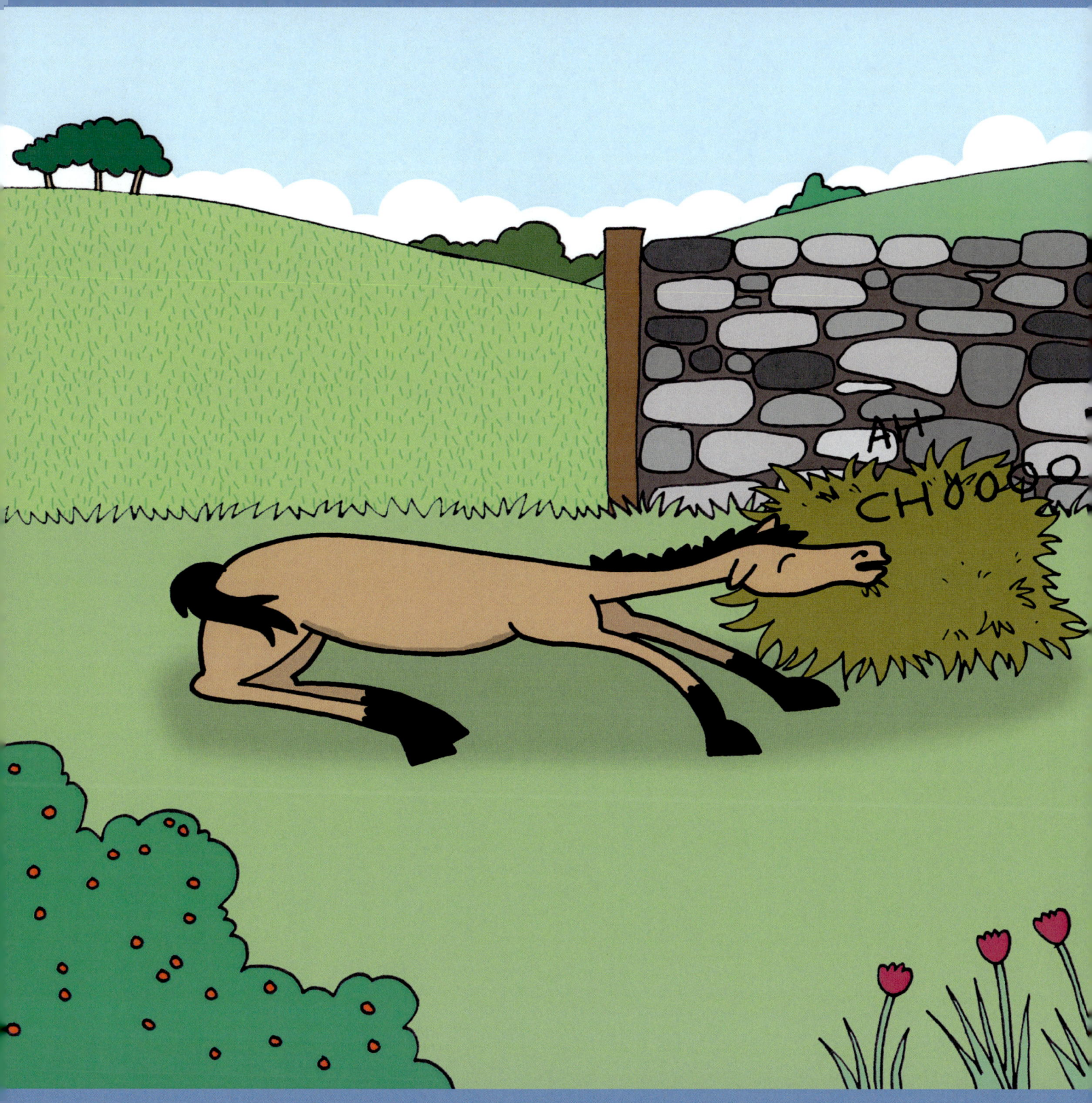

"I want a fluffy pillow." He snorted.

He even tried a moss covered
log, but it was home to a noisey
bull frog!

"I WANT A FLUFFY PILLOW!"
Paxton whinnied.

"Let's go home, son." His parents called.

"But i need a fluffy pillow." Paxton sobbed. They trotted

They trotted home. Paxton had looked everywhere for a fluffy pillow.

After all his adventures Paxton still hadn't found a fluffy pillow.

Then he walked into his stall ....

"A FLUFFY PILLOW!" Paxton
cheered.

There was a note that said,
"Love Grandma."

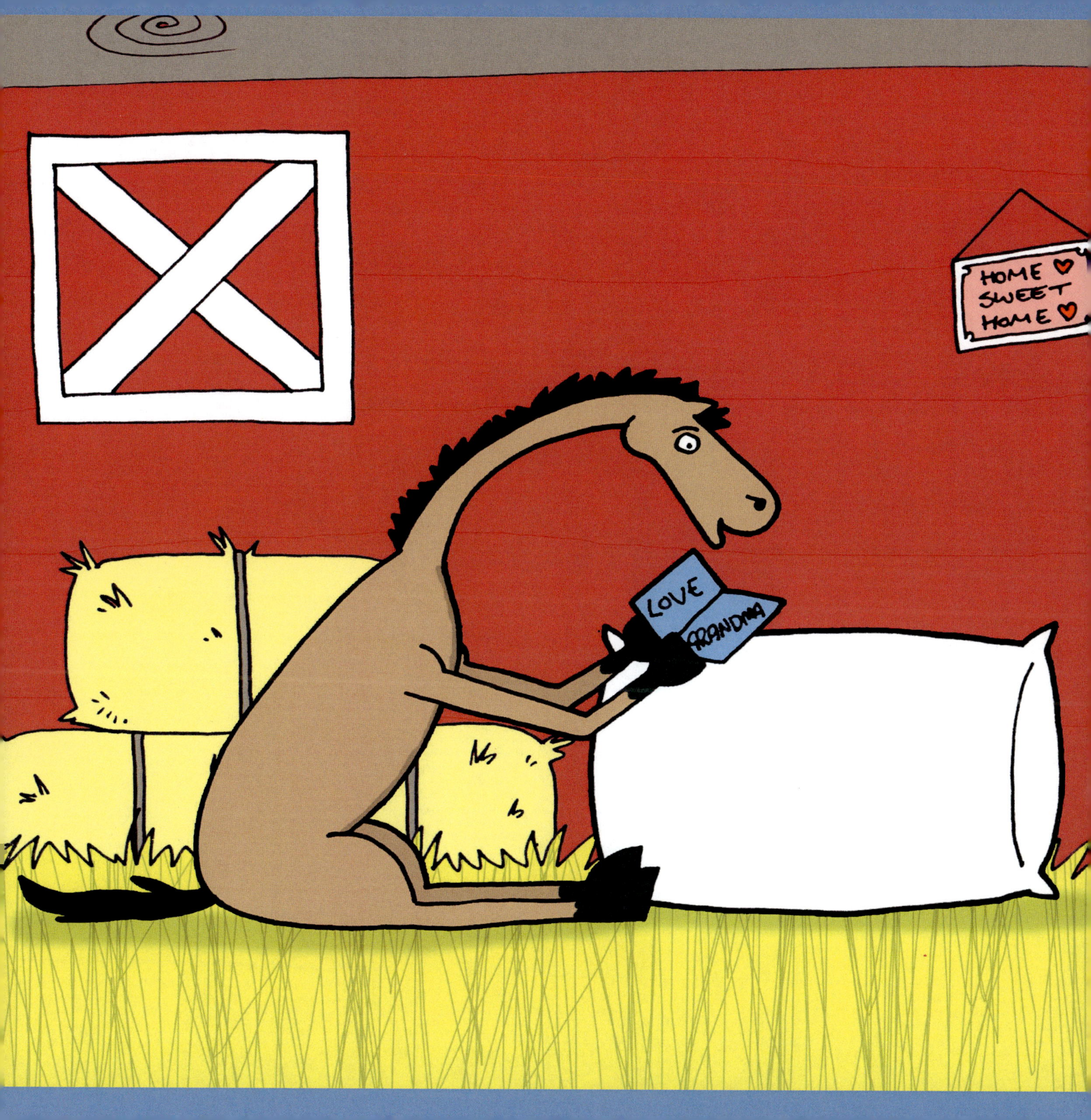
HOME
SWEET
HOME
LOVE
GRANDMA

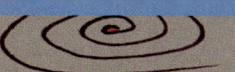

Paxton flopped on his new fluffy pillow and was soon sound asleep.

Made in the USA
Middletown, DE
31 October 2025

19534972R00024